Find the Odd One
for Kids

Edwin Kim

Ilustrated by
Mayara Nogueira

COPYRIGHT © ASCEND DIGITAL LLC
ALL RIGHTS RESERVED

Can you find the odd one? Can you spot them all? Get your eyes and mind ready to start looking! Invite your family and friends to join in on the fun!

CAN YOU FIND THE ODD ONE OUT?

CAKE

IS THE ONE ODD ONE OUT!

PENCIL

IS THE ONE ODD ONE OUT!

CAN YOU FIND THE ODD ONE OUT?

SNEAKERS

IS THE ONE ODD ONE OUT!

DOLL

IS THE ONE ODD ONE OUT!

CAN YOU FIND THE ODD ONE OUT?

SCHOOLBAG

IS THE ONE ODD ONE OUT!

SWEATER

IS THE ONE ODD ONE OUT!

TEDDY BEAR

IS THE ONE ODD ONE OUT!

CHEESE

IS THE ONE ODD ONE OUT!

GLOVES

IS THE ONE ODD ONE OUT!

BOOK

IS THE ONE ODD ONE OUT!

BALL

IS THE ONE ODD ONE OUT!

CAN YOU FIND THE ODD ONE OUT?

PANCAKES

IS THE ONE ODD ONE OUT!

CAN YOU FIND THE ODD ONE OUT?

SANDWICH

IS THE ONE ODD ONE OUT!

PENCIL CASE

IS THE ONE ODD ONE OUT!

CAP

IS THE ONE ODD ONE OUT!

CAN YOU FIND THE ODD ONE OUT?

ROBOT

IS THE ONE ODD ONE OUT!

PANTS

IS THE ONE ODD ONE OUT!

COOKIES

IS THE ONE ODD ONE OUT!

CAN YOU FIND THE ODD ONE OUT?

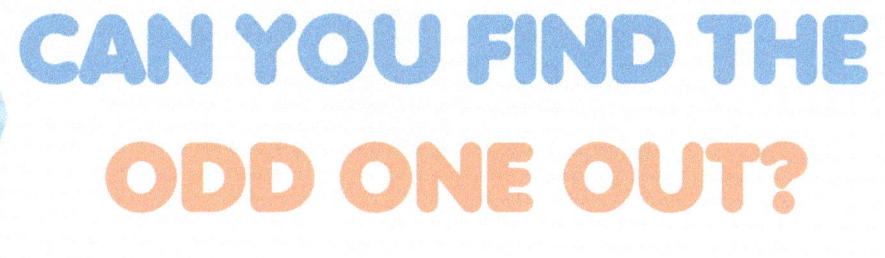

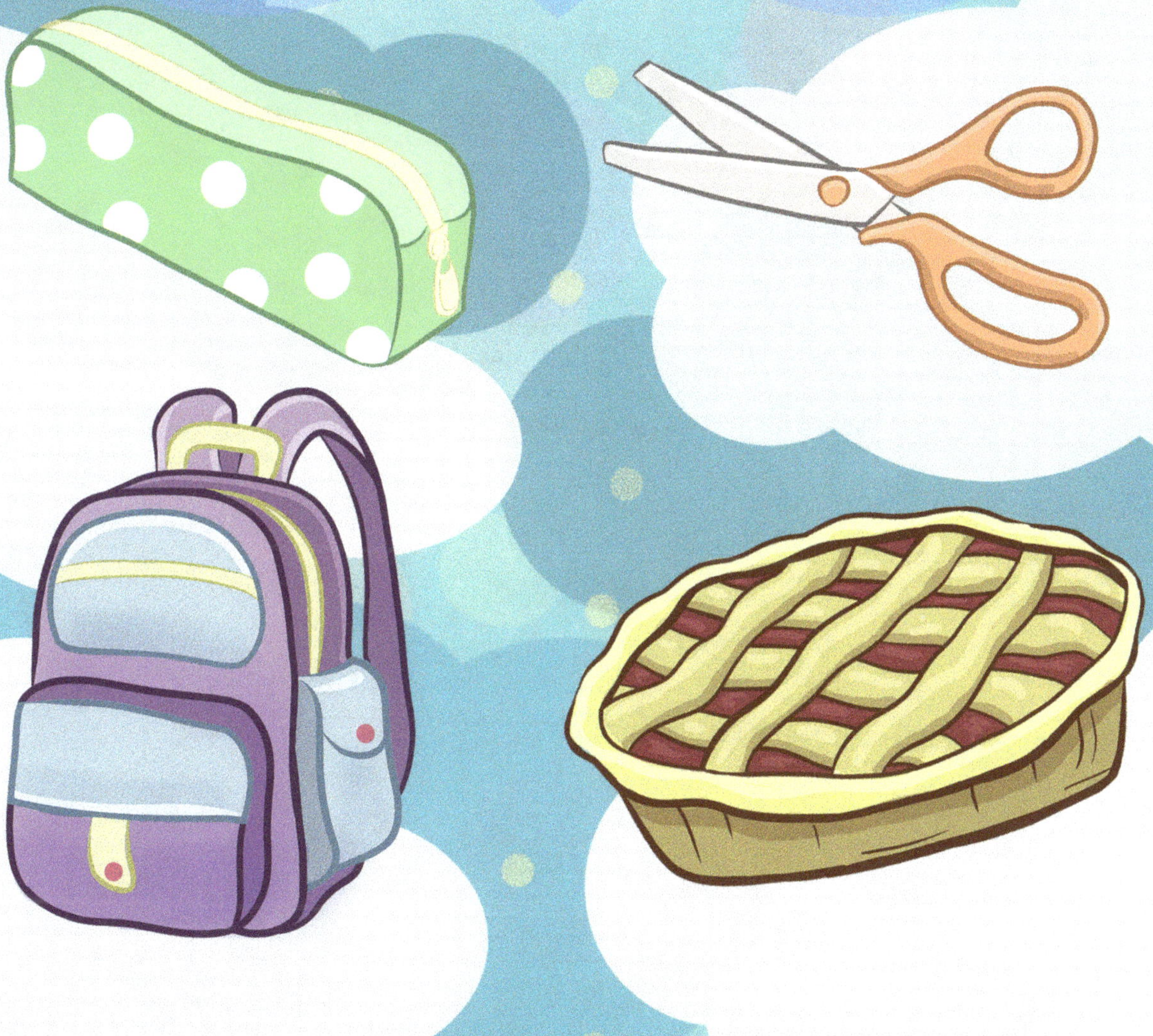

PIE

IS THE ONE ODD ONE OUT!

Author
Edwin Kim
edwinkim.co

Edwin Kim is a creative entrepreneur who loves to create inspirational books that can bring valuable lessons to the next generation. He happily creates stories and loves to bring his ideas to life.

Ilustrator
Mayara Nogueira
artstation.com/mayaranogueira

Mayara is passionate about the world of illustrated books. She loves drawing animals, historical and fantasy themes.

www.ingramcontent.com/pod-product-compliance
Lightning Source LLC
Chambersburg PA
CBHW051121110526
44589CB00026B/2994